MW01383953

# The Brevity of Red

# The Brevity of Red

## Jill MacLean

*Jill MacLean* (signature)

George Amabile, Editor

Signature
EDITIONS

Cover design by Terry Gallagher/Doowah Design.
Cover photo by Tracey L. Sneesby.
Photo of Jill MacLean by Joel Ross Photography.

This book was printed on Ancient Forest Friendly paper.
Printed and bound in Canada by AGMV Marquis Imprimeur Inc.

We acknowledge the support of The Canada Council for the Arts and the Manitoba Arts Council for our publishing program.

National Library of Canada Cataloguing in Publication Data

MacLean, Jill, 1941–
        The brevity of red / Jill MacLean.

Poems.
ISBN 0-921833-92-X

                I. Title.

PS8575.L415B74 2003          C811'.6          C2003-903761-4

Signature Editions
P.O. Box 206, RPO Corydon, Winnipeg, Manitoba, R3M 3S7

*for Colin*

# Contents

# Time Change

I stop the third hand's radar
sweep, make the little hand
subtract 1. The hour isn't
fractured into metacarpals and

phalanges; it's cupped, held
whole and open, the head
of a newborn. It's a fuzzy
neon tennis ball, a wandering

mandarin, a deerhide drum
tapped by polished knuckle
bones. It isn't, I insist,
the brown-rimmed heart

of a barn owl's face with its flesh-
pink beak, its black eyes socketed
in the softest of white
feathers. Once, it was

in Dominica, I saw the full
moon magnified 80X. Saw
the flawed and faulted in their
luminosity. Is the hour like

the rocks on Gooseberry
Beach, curved and cool
to the hand? The brawl
that shapes them. (I'd rather

the hour be a new notebook,
the pages parabolas
of emptiness.) Later
we found battlements

built with the rocks,
bunkers hollowed from them.
Systematically executed. Facing
the sea. The house

sparrows clamped
to the rungs of the feeder
know the slow increase
of darkness, the decrease

of everything else. They know
that in a strong wind the tops
of spruce trees swing
into orbit; couldn't care less

that a restless universe
shoulders the galaxies this way
and that (never outward
because there's no

centre). I can't give the hour
away. You already have one,
and besides, in 6 months it will be
snatched back. But for now

the hour is mine and purple
like Hella Lacey asters named by
a philosopher who gardens
in the fall. Greedy like

blouses pegged in the wind,
their biceps straining
for the last rose: Henry Hudson, icy-
white – cast adrift, who died

first, father or son? Joyous
like the dog who corkscrews
in the middle of Duffus Street, lunges
for Needham Hill, shrubby Louvre

of odours. Were I blind and deaf,
my nostrils would tell me
if I stood beside an ocean
or a pond. This hour smells of

manumission, complex
as allspice, alchemical as
compost. I go out into the garden.
I don't come in till dark.

# Chaconne

I crouch among standing stones
    where a woman holds a death mask high
        foxfire and marshfire glow
            through holes where the eyes were
                through the ruined mouth

I'm spellbound by the cut-faced cliff
    where a woman holds a death mask high
        blue winds of the sea lure me
            through spinning eyes
                and plangent mouth

I'm drenched within this fragrant glade
    where a woman holds a death mask high
        sorrel and yarrow blooming
            through its stretched eyes
                soiled mouth

I stand fast under an opaque sky
    where a woman holds a death mask high
        rosefinches and white owls flow
            through its far-seeking eyes
                its mouth shapely with song

# A Stranger in the House

I wish I'd written poems when my daughter
was young. Making wine from dandelions,

I might have glimpsed how heroism
can be quiet, like a child's breathing.

I have no pencilled scraps, confetti
of an ordinary life. In an old photograph

she stands beside her daughter, this woman
with my name; I invent dialogue,

embroider the minutes cushioning
that split second. The woman stares at the one

who transfixed her. She dreams of rescue,
polishes the furniture so no fingerprints

remain. She loves her daughter
inarticulately, fears a baby might be

as easily dismembered as a doll:
anoints with lotion, offers oats and milk,

knits scarves that curl inward
tense with prayer. She picks a sheaf

of lupins, bringing aphids into the house;
month after month, watches ravens

enter the openwork of boughs. On the wall,
inked lines show how her daughter grows.

driving in winter, after the accident

*blood*
*of a*
*wounded*
*deer*

    red dirt
    on the white
    shoulder of the road

*wing*
*of a*
*dead*
*crow*

    tattered
    fragment
    of a tire

it will take years
for the similes of healing:

that clod of earth
is like the body of a raccoon

that body of a raccoon
is like a clod of earth

# I Wish This Whole Poem Were a Dream

You're standing beside my bed,
wrapped in earth-
stained bandages.
An end is loose. I wait
for you to unravel,

blinded and silenced daughter

Blue-flowered shower cap
on your head, your fingernails
dirty. The doctors
will revoke
the rise and fall of your chest,

daughter in limbo

At your grave the ground
has sunk, gapes like
the kind of wound from which
bowels spill. What can I do
but poultice with red valley clay,

corporeal daughter

Walking to the Appletree
Café – gold dress, lemon dress,
like coltsfoot in spring – we talk
about sex; and my mother
(my long-dead mother) fails to shame me
into silence, turns her back, curls
her bones like a fetus,

ripe daughter

On this sunny day in August – black
skirt, fuchsia blouse – I follow you
down the aisle. I lie with you
for months, I beat against
the coffin lid, flinch
from the too-strong light
that we call love,

daughter

# That First Year

your brother walks alone
to the school bus

two butterflies, paler
than the yellow hawkweed, dance
up and up into the dying elm

the orchard is spattered red

tide and wind are siblings of the bay,
maple leaves twist in the sun; last night's
chill painted the grass white
between the graves

I need a stone in place
before the snow

for fear of losing you

the morning mist is pallid: snow
rising from its place of rest

trees stand like a row of monks
their praise as cool as indrawn breath

from suppliant branches, the birds herald
this false spring, so gentle, so riddled with deceit

your brother
never mentions your name,
doubling the absence
of a presence so strong
we still don't
eat at a table set for two

last summer's weeds
collapse in the ice-fed river

and everywhere the skin
splits open on the bud

among dusty catkins
a song sparrow practices his *yes*



your brother and I pay
attention to the tense
of verbs...*would have been*
for high school graduation



meadow rue, forget-me-nots, bleeding heart's pink and white lockets
foxgloves that cure the heart, monkshood that poisons it
snow-in-summer, bee balm, pearly everlasting
                                    an avalanche of roses



eleven months
since I've heard your voice
or had a glimpse of you
and in the cemetery at dusk
in the quietest of visions
I see women in worn brown robes
and blue shawls: mourners,
tenders of graves, they keep
a courteous distance

they've wandered
through the damp grass
from an orchard of unripe apples,
which, in some way
not yet divined,
I'm to bring to fruition

# Hannah's Lament for Her Son, Samuel

Sundown. Low clouds red as the pomegranates
whose sweet, slippery seeds I crammed into my mouth
my second month. Dust around the donkeys' hooves. Wind
in the terebinth grove – they say women used to worship there.
　　　We're nearly home.

I remember the midwife gripping my hands, Samuel's head
jammed between my legs as I heaved for air, bleating
like a ewe...How he loved to toss coloured stones
from the stream – they shone like little fish. For years
　　　I was barren.

Elkanah rides ahead of me. He took greasy-haired Peninnah
to his bed, cow that yearly drops a calf. When I first
lay with him, he said my wrists were like the wingbones
of a quail. A woman without children is a branch of thorns
　　　on her husband's pillow.

At the well, I had no stories of new teeth and sudden tumbles.
And every year – as now – a pilgrimage to Shiloh. Bitterness
travelled with me, wormwood that lingers in the pasture.
"Why do you weep?" he cried. "Aren't I more to you
　　　than ten sons?"

One year I walked alone into the temple, my heartbeat
like a goat's dragged to the altar. *You closed my womb. I am
cracked earth and shrivelled wheat.* "Grant me, Your maidservant,
a son," I said, "and I will give him to Your service all the days
　　　of his life."

I should have remembered Peninnah, how when her babe
is placed in her arms she's beautiful, as though a lamp
lights her from within. The Lord heard my vow.
My bleeding stopped. Within me grew the son
　　　who wasn't mine.

When he quickened, I was a swallow skimming fields
of cornflowers. Apricots, softly furred, fell into my basket. Elkanah
ground the wheat for me. Peninnah washed her hair with lemons.
Then the slow clenching of my belly, like ropes tightening
　　　around a donkey's load.

Samuel's eyes, blue-black, filled me with such love
as I have never known. He played all day rough as a lion cub,
at night sought the den of my embrace. And then my breasts
dried up. Once again – this morning, early – I stood
        in Shiloh's temple,


I said, "I am returning my son to the Lord." It's past Samuel's
bedtime. Is he crying for me in the dark? I make a second vow:
never again to force my way into God's story. Let other women
be the mothers of prophets, priests and kings.
        Let other women be the mothers.


Peninnah has placed a lamp
in the east window
to welcome us home.

it hasn't rained for many days

though my throat is sealed
        and my skin cracking, I leave
the sunken river, lope toward the hemlocks,

press my ear, my breast, my belly
        to one of the old ones –
the wind's collisions fill my skull.

roots, thick-wristed, claw into decay,
        the crown leans to the rising sun,
can be used as a compass

– I sing an incendiary
        song, hurl sparks far
into the woods' tinder –

seedlings of jack pine will push
        through the earth's blackened flank
like rough green fur.

# Milking

          After the phone call,
the membranes of my cells
dissolve, *prognosis nil*
encroaches on every nucleus.
Years since you were weaned.

          You travel
the black spindles of division
until I no longer listen for you scraping
mud from your boots; until grief's
not a snake eating its tail, but a kettling

          of hawks. Meanwhile,
you fragment into memories. Cast
ox-eyed daisies in the hole, revise
their petalled litany. Trickle words
on the smooth wood:

          a teenager herds
Holsteins; lets cool, silky grain
slip through her fingers. She clangs
stanchions shut, vaults electric
fences. Unalterably altered,

          I know there is no ground
to stand on. You stood on wooden steps
where hay dust flirted with light.
You wanted each barn cat
to have its milk.

## haiku from a perennial garden

unfolding its white
petals takes the peony
an entire morning

# Of All the Eventualities

*you're running down the lane*
*late for the school bus*
*brown hair swinging*

                    Once, on
the MacDonald Bridge — you were telling me
about your job, how you scrubbed mud and dung
from the flanks of Holsteins,
you were describing their enormous bones,
the sleekly aligned hairs, completely white
or black — you nearly drove into
a van that braked
ahead of you. Once, in a parking lot,
you backed into a pickup truck.

You crammed the hours
that summer. I'd find you
asleep in the afternoon
under flowered sheets, their careless
marigolds.
                    You went blueberry picking,
drove my car across the yellow lines.
Ripe berries. Broken glass.

Guilt isn't as it sounds, clipped, pale gold.

Years later, I'm driving the highway where
it happened, the wiper clearing my view
on both sides of its pivot — *bad driver,*
*good driver* — for the first time
I wonder if you were merely
an average driver:

a bell-shaped curve, a womb
for the absorption of extremes.

How many mothers toss a daughter the car keys,
later find her back home, asleep
on the couch?
                    Does the mother conclude
she's a good mother? No, she wonders
if she'll risk Colombian coffee before bed,
or stick with almond sunset tea.

To our countless actions, we ascribe
so little weight
when they don't end in disaster.


*you turn around in the lane*
*you're running toward me*

# Beloved Grotesque

Your gills seal shut. You're pushed
beyond fish, and — once my waters
break — into the air.

The tidal pool, dependable the whole summer
that you're two — you're half in water,
half in air — that great salt lake,
the prolonged sighing
past the range of sand. Sea trout
slippery in your father's net, do you see
only silver backflips and not
the desperation? Do you remember
capelin funnelling to the estuary, so many
they're flung upon the shore?

Thin straps over your swimmer's shoulders
held the weight of your breasts.
You were driving — highway
shimmering in the heat —
until your eyes swam with sleep.

Do we bury the young as though the earth
were water, wait for them to come up
for air? After your tumbleturns, you surged
from the end walls of the pool,
palms to thighs and toes pointed, bubbles
tasselling through turquoise.

Twenty years have passed. I go
on the assumption that bones
are what's left: fossae and foramina, your once-
supple spine. The rest of you propels
hydrogen through the mitochondria
of root hairs, sends out small flares
from the yellow rafts
of dandelions. My loafers
lapped by the grass beside your grave,
I breathe in the pleasures
of blue sky:
                    you're still anchored,
you can't entirely float away.

# Latticework

The windows of the white church are poised
like warheads. Once there were farms here.

Helices of possibility haul apart;
I shall hang an ox yoke on the wall.

What *is* a nuclear family? Flowers
are linked by the singing trails of wasps.

Breaking of the waters – my viscera evicted –
there'll be nothing left!

My fingers curl around broken glass,
lantern moss. Tiger lilies erupt

from the foundations. Who is she, clear
as the sun, terrible as an army with banners?

Shout to the hills like a barred owl –
sometimes a barred owl will reply.

What is *accident* but a pebble on the long trail
of cause and effect? Rocks molten in the river,

light whipping a drowned quarry. In Grise Fjord,
night lasts three months; ravens are invisible.

Try looking into your own pupils: no pigment,
just darkness. Over the drowned, the spectrum

rends. The stems of wood lilies,
hollow with longing.

Is this what's meant by *watershed* – my daughter
dead as many years as she was alive?

The cellist plays Fauré's *Elegy*.
Lost, and found.

Dismantle rabbit snares. Pray your children avoid
steel traps by watercourses.

Loosed over a cliff – quick
sunlight, buntings white as spume.

Leaf shadows drowsy on leaves. "To see an image,"
Tu Fu is told, "is like being alive twice."

So agreeable, that low hedge of basil.
Rotted manure, the antonym for *meagre*.

I'll plant something deep-rooted;
stroking the leaves, I'll touch her bones.

Woodsmoke drifts through the birches.
To follow the scent of your own burning.

# Son

He's on highway patrol.

Blue sky, west wind, crows
reeling. White-outs
thick as summer fog, without
fog's consolation.

He's first on the scene.

He sees how the gun was cleaned and oiled,
how the inner life of a man
glistens on the bathroom tiles.
He leaves the wife at the neighbours' –
"I didn't know," she keeps saying –
and goes back
to take the required photographs. After
the ambulance has left, he finds a pail
under the sink, wipes the tiles clean.

He adjudicates right from wrong.

Bland curves of snow, cover-up
of detail. The insistent
trees, their shadows accurate and wildly
inaccurate.

He believes in common sense.

Tell the truth, he tells his son: hope
and love, in the usual way, conspiring to his undoing.
At the rink he plays defence, drinks
more than one beer when his team wins the trophy. His son
wears the same gear in miniature.

He keeps the peace.

He investigates beagles that howl at midnight, the theft
from the thrift shop, drunks who smash
empties of Black Horse
into scalpels of glass. So far,
he hasn't been called out
for a child.

He remembers the first time he said,
"Lean on the car with your hands flat on the roof,"
and the man did.

On his belt: gun, cuffs, baton, radio.
His integument of discretion toughens to silence.
Three settings on his siren: hi-lo, yelp
and wail.

Off-duty, he follows the shoreline
on his snowmobile. Back
to the trees, he lights his camp stove, brews tea.
Pack ice jammed in the strait: a chaotic
stillness: he couldn't have deduced
the great movements of tides.

# Sojourn

Jays wheedle the last blue
into the shadowed
pines. Chickadees puncture
the brittle air, blurring
the snow's belly, the grey wings
of sky. Spruce trees creep closer, bled
of green, afflicted with crows.

Daylight, extravagant, loosed
grosbeaks plump as sunflowers,
finches the colour of raspberries.

Fed so bounteously, imagination
will not, at dusk, go peaceably
to roost. The birds of darkness hunch
at the window, tap the glass.

# Fledgling

He's stolen galvanized nails and three pine boards
for the fort he's building in the woods

but he's been told to water the beans and pick
potato beetles, their brown-striped uniforms.

He drops them on a rock, bayonets them with a twig.
A starling, fledged from the second brood

in the rain gutter, blunders toward him,
stops, hypnotized by the drip of the hose.

He picks it up, excited by the feathered scrape
against his thumb, the wiry, futile claws. He nails

the bird down low to the back of the shed.
The parents scream, diving him as he swings

the hammer in awkward arcs – did he hesitate
as he spread the first wing against the shingle –

is there always or ever a pause, in which forbearance
can draw breath – the fledgling's panting, he sees

its tongue. When his brother calls him for supper, he hides
the boards, tucks the starling under the squash vines'

brassy trumpets. He sprays his hands
with the hose, and runs for home.

# In Alabaster for the Palace of the King of Assyria

*in low relief*

your apprentices carve trees like
pineapples, citizens of Nineveh
hurrying for the best view of

the arena's whips
and deep-ribbed mastiffs,
stallions who look like they'd rather be elsewhere

the lions' manes layered like artichoke leaves
*their claws hooked, their knuckles muscled*

the slats on the cages sinuous as rivers: wildness
(you know this) writhes against confinement

*lioness curled around her triad of arrows, her tributaries of blood*

the king,, portly and serene, stars
sprinkling his dress, the cosmos
on his side as he stretches
his bow or angles his spear

the guards, not a hair out of place

*lion thrashing at the arrow that enters his eye, splits his tongue*

out of the question to chisel a king who
grunts as he throws all his weight
into rupturing hide and viscera —

*lioness, disembowelled, drags her haunches*
you shape her eyes like drops of water

in his stone chariot, the king smiles
into a nothing that's far away

when the last panel's finished, he gives
an order: from the stumps
your blood carves channels in the sand

# The Brevity of Red

From indoors, I watch the redpoll
settle into the snow as though brooding

eggs, her eyelids thin white lines. Later
she falls on her side, her claws gripping

a white sky, crown feathers a lively
crimson. Below the photograph

of a concrete wall splashed a sticky red,
lines of print where the bodies must have

fallen. Not even from a distance could this red
be mistaken for the velvet-gown-in-winter

red of chrysanthemums blooming against
stone steps. Every day, on the screen,

we see the faces of those whose flesh
has been laid open. Here

the year goes from green to brown
to white to brown to green.

# Outside my double-glazed window

28 below, wind chill minus 40: this is how
quickly heat is stripped from the skin. Inside,
*Schefflera;* a thick-trunked jade; *Maranta*
and *Monstera deliciosa*, its glossy, riddled
leaves. And amaryllis, each bloom a bowl
glazed salmon, lime and white, luscious
as a contralto.
         Wearing a balaclava
like men who throw stones at their oppressors
I hurry to my night class past posters stapled
over boarded windows. At the takeout,
feral cats crack bones. A man with Tourette's
works the bus stop, I drop coins into his plastic cup.
Scabs on his lip; his companion bundled
in cardboard. Why wouldn't they
break the two panes, feed
their fires with my books, with the planks
under the books,
         with wood of the jade?

# A Few Days after the Whirlwind

"But now I see You with my eyes."
Job 42:5

God seized me, spun me, dropped me
as the vulture drops jackal bones
to reach the marrow.
                    Brass-jawed Behemoth mauled
my gullet. Blood glugged like olive oil from a jug.

Last week's fingers pustuled, now
they're smooth, resting on my tunic of fine wool.
Rocks knotted under me – I still get dizzy, standing. Down
in the valley, my house, the sheds and fields. Sheep
penned for the shearing. Camels, oxen, donkeys –

twice what I owned before.
One wife, though. The same seven sons, three daughters,
they woke unstartled from their dream of death. My first words,
afterward, an act of naming. Cinnamon,
Dove, Eye-Shadow.

I saw God's shadow. I see It still.
Mustard sun in a sky of flax. A hail of white anemones.

You've heard about the ash heap? Like a cockerel
confident of sunrise, I pecked the boundary stones
of blasphemy, spurred the heavens for a hearing
(better the stew pot at a simmer).
God spoke:

*Hidden blossoms of the fig tree bearing fruit*
*in three seasons.*
*Puffed and tufted running and ridiculous*
*ostrich. Bloody nostrils of wild*
*poppies, ice*
*in the eagle's talons. A burnt offering*
*of wrens, a prayer shawl of hornets.*
*The deep,* tehom, *the wasteland,* tohu.

And nowhere us.
　　　　　Only the chaotic whirl
of our pronged and hungry alphabet before God inhaled
*aleph* and *bet,* proclaimed evening, morning and the rule of man.
　　　　　How I despised

the broken fingernails of the poor, the widow's
whine, the mucus and the stink. I yoked God
to a wooden plough, made Him plod the furrow,
bled ram after ram and lived in dread.
And now?

I've broken the law – I've given my daughters
an inheritance.
The faces of my sons like
　　　　boulders.
My wife won't touch a man God-riven.

Yesterday, timorous as a coney in my frayed brown robe,
　　　　　I climbed the hillside, crossed the gully. The outcasts
scuttled into crevices. I left honeycombs
　　　　and curdled goat's milk, whispered
that I would return.

The life of the vole feathers the falcon; who, broken-winged
in a cowl of vultures, screams for his own life.

The white lilies of the mountain send out their scent by night.

# Ear to the Ground

His fisted silences. Yet the yellow primrose
offered itself completely.

Lupins, hooded and slit — why was she made
in the image of a flower?

Watercolours don't allow revision. She hangs
a prayer plant in an obscure corner; learns

murre eggs are pointed, won't roll off a cliff.
After his suicide, her one-voiced quarrel.

*The tongue of my ravings in my ear*
*is the tongue of a stranger.*

Ravel's *Kaddish*: the piano's small stones.
The violin's disconsolate wanderings.

The sky — blue-walled womb
for the deformities of love, its perfect fingernails.

Whose heartbeat does she hear?
The fibrillations of what she could never say?

Inside the yellow fruit, red lattice of mace,
speckled nutmeg. Her lover, a polisher of surfaces.

She floats, belly-up, past the ruins of the sea,
an oriole between her breasts.

Pelvic bones like an urn, ash drifting
into her garden, its rococo delphiniums.

*Oh Lord, encompass me.* Peach sunlight
on one side of the branches.

When spruce trees gather night into themselves,
it is the most natural of gestures.

She buys a dictionary of etymology:
boulder from *bullersten,*

thunderstone. The stone is lost,
the faraway roar remains.

She meets the blue gaze of an infant, watches
an Arctic poppy tilt toward the sun.

And when she rubs the rim of her Tibetan singing bowl,
sound hangs like a horizon, trembling.

# Composed in Exile

Giya Kancheli's music, he says, fills a space
that has been deserted. Inanimate, flickering

granite; a feather lying to one side of the track. Wind
from the Caucasus lifts the feather, lets it fall.

He calls his prayer cycle *Life without Christmas.*
My firstborn tastes dry white light, then

the cord is cut: it is now possible for her
to drown. Sound carries over water. Over

ice. Over the river's new geography of dead-end
creeks and soft, grey swamps. Why is the space

deserted? He bends to scrutinize the ground where
the hated and the haters lie. Notes of a clarinet

slide among them; a boy sings *Domine,*
*exaudi vocem meam.* Andromeda rushes toward us.

After her birth, I tremble
among animals, walk in the snow

beside the tracks of a red fox. Earlier —
or later — a vole crossed the path. In the villages

of Georgia, how many woke
to fists pounding the door?

*Abii me videram*…how many
turn away so as not to see?

I have seen whooping cranes feeding
through broken ice. Without love,

I am a sounding cymbal, *forze e barbaro.*
To share the broth in which the last wedge of cabbage

was boiled. Look at the eyes. At the teeth. Fragments
of folk songs. The women forgot *asiatic* and

*Turk's cap,* forgot *lily.* My children
are not among the disappeared.

Snow melts around tree trunks as though they were
warm-blooded. His attenuated notes, his *pianissimos*

are like winter trees, birds' nests no longer
hidden. From blue sky falls

a mauve rain of wisteria;
in the museum, the Stradivarius

is locked away –
do you sit on a train facing the past,

or the future? The shade of buildings
differs from the shade of trees.

In his prayers for the night, hear how
the saxophone cauterizes grief.

## Volunteer

Asked to visit a woman
from Kyushu who is as lost
in my language as I

in hers, whose husband
and sons are tired of her
dying, I discover she's

tall, her head like
an overblown peony
so thinly stalked

a rainshower would bow it
to the ground, her skin
smooth as an old ivory

Buddha in the pocket of
a beggar who writes
many haiku – and although

neither of us knows
what to do, on the second day
she shivers, her fingers

brushing her feet,
which are large and flat,
formed for the courtesies

of karate-dō, and so cold
I rub her fallen arches,
her swollen ankles,

whereupon she weeps
with very little sound,
her forehead on my shoulder

like a small stone lantern,
causing me to wonder if
when we drop words

into silence — cries of
cuckoos through bamboo
empty of listeners —

we fail other silences, we
fail the tendons that give
the fingers their clasp.

# Late in March

I'm walking by the river. Cottonwoods and ash
overhang cold mud, the lack of stones. Inch by inch,

flood plain emerges from the snow; soon
the buteos' incisions in the sky. My first week

in this city. But the man walking toward me,
surely that's – the man's a stranger, nods, passes by.

All day I've been expecting my mother to phone,
although it's forty years since she died. More

and more, the people I meet remind me of people
I have already met: similarity arm in arm

with difference, which is my hope for the world.
Hopeless. But I'm walking by the river. The dogwoods'

winter scarlet turns toward introspection. Soon ice
from the south will sail past, the muddy water

will smell like the river I waded when I was nine,
poked at with a stick. Gingham skirts tucked

into my knickers. My mother took a photo of me
from behind, entered it in a contest.

Even then I was poking at opacity,
wading through it to get where I was going.

# Locked-In Syndrome

Stroke: a blow to the brain. Your body
lolled, disobedient as I'd never dared to be.
Wrinkled sheets you couldn't smooth,
your throat a paralysis of syllables.

I brought my wedding dress and veil,
my fragile plans, offering them
to you and the hospital clock that knocked
on the black barrier of each second. Your breath

like rotting peaches. In the sepia photograph,
your hand on my father's sleeve, your body
leans away, ivy from your bouquet snags
his knees. He gave you a cameo brooch, a nymph

on the run, pinned it to your lapel. War posters
warning against idle talk. The boy I played with
after the war, the yellow fountain he made
under the weeping willow – his name, the brass

seven-branched candlestick, years before
I realized – and who was the Russian woman
who boarded with us all one winter? I dreamed
of limp rubber gas masks, of queues assembling

in the blackout, the women's pale faces, pale
waiting hands. A man in Berck-sur-Mer, immobilized
like you, blinks his left eyelid to a spoken
alphabet, letter by letter writes a book. Could we

have done the same? Spell *yes*. Spell
*claustrophobia*. Your evening gown cobalt
like delphiniums, each sequin a blue
mirror, *mother* a discarded housedress.

Twice you overwintered English wallflowers,
their alchemy of rust and fire. Vegetables
at the back of your garden. Love never spoken of.
Long after you were dead, I questioned your sisters,

who said: "she wouldn't try an avocado; I made her
a black hat with ostrich feathers and she never
thanked me; she had a miscarriage – or was it
an abortion? she was a cold woman; she was our father's

favourite; your father, before they were married –
he drove an old red motorbike –
gave her a silk shawl that shimmered in the light...
they went for a day trip on the Channel,

she was seasick and the shawl
ruined." The sisters, too, are dead.
As for you, could you have looked at your life
aslant, or were you kept too busy scalding,

slicing and ironing it? You followed
your husband to Canada, every Sunday
made Yorkshire puddings
that depended on emptiness to rise.

...sit on a cushion and sew a fine seam

tissue pattern, dark blue
print. her non-standard shape
to be negotiated, pins
like little silver
flagpoles. darts
concede breasts
and waist. thread's
protective coloration.
the skirt flares.

the old Singer
intertwines thread from above
with thread from below: stitches
facings to the collar, which
now encircles her throat.
the hem is as straight as a ruler.

watch her scissors
parting the material.
the oak table
appears like a dark
arrow, the cut
irreversible
as time: which
she's trying to fashion
so it becomes her.

haiku from behind the house

  October wind –
the chained dog cannot
   follow his nose

# Yizhaq, Which Means Laughter

Behold – I'm Isaac, son of Abraham.
My deathbed a tent of black goats' hair
rain-sodden. Winter clatter of the palms.
I'm toothless, blind and lizard-skinned: for years
the women bring me lentil stew, hot bread
from the stones. My father's eyes the rope that
held me down, knife hanging like a hawk,
a brutal sun (after, I used to trap larks
and break their wings). And then? Ram-stink, the cut
fumbled, my father mute. Geese scrape the reeds,
settle on their eggs. My wife's twin sons –
my seven brothers, ten and seven grandsons.
I lie on the split wood of my old bones,
a copper link in the Lord's chain of bronze.

# The Day after Father's Day

*It's water under the bridge*…rough beams
over field runoff, a magnet for the rusty

splinters of swallows. *Estranged*
implies I treated you as a stranger.

No. I was too adamant.
We were raccoons, masked, clawed

and ingenious. Now that you're dead,
other old men shuffle down the street,

their eyes afloat under distorting
lenses. Why didn't I snap

the precisions of your slide rule, yellowed
like the nicotine on your fingers –

I wanted you cruising Mykonos, planting
swirls of Orange Wonder tulips. Once,

you came to stay with me, tripped
over a cord. The lamp crashed to the floor.

"That's not a good beginning," you said.
In the nursing home, you swept the air

with your stick. "Why can't I go
to Florida?" A snapshot from your mediocre

boarding school: your mouth clamped, desk
gouged. Your father an inventor and a drinker,

not to be counted on for holidays. Years later,
I knitted you diamond socks in your school colours –

sky-blue, red and purple – and you wore them.
You apprenticed as an aeronautical designer;

young and able-bodied,
you took the train to and from work

for the six years of the war. You were sole
provider for a family of four; held

lively conversations with yourself.
When I came to tell you my sister, your daughter

had died, you said, "I feel lonely." The only
words from the heart you ever spoke to me and

I left, left quickly, left you alone. Grief
is a burden; regret goes backward

through weeping toward speech. You
retched as you eviscerated our wartime,

fondly named hens. Near the end,
I fed you creamed chicken. "I love you,"

I said, from across the private room,
the words flavourless yet firm. You replied

in kind. It was a formality. Swallows drink
on the wing from water the colour of their nests.

# Father-in-Law

The winter he's twenty-seven,
he and his second cousin Harvey walk
North Sydney to Ingonish. "Ninety-seven
miles," he says. "We'd been working
the supply boat but she got froze in."
A wife at home with three sons,
a fourth child due, no other way back.

Late afternoon they're taken in and fed
salt herring, molasses cookies and tea
strong enough to walk on. For miles
they follow deer tracks that clip the snow
neat as pliers. A yellow
bullet hole where it peed.

At nightfall, they share a plug of Old Sailor.
"Remember the feller in Hake's Cove
who drowned his wife in the well
and kept right on drinking the water?"

They shiver pleasurably. A fir bough claws
his sleeve, the moon's up and
round as a snare. The less a rabbit
struggles, the slower it dies.

Stars flash — lighthouses
whose keepers talk only
to themselves. At home when he treks
to the outhouse before bed, the stars are
comfortable, the pattern on an old dinner plate.

The wedding photo on their bureau, the bony
outcrops of his forehead. He looks straight
through the camera to all the work he has to do
by winter. Two days past his twentieth birthday.

Before that, he spent long slow days on the water,
a planed sea, curls of wake. Scanning from the mast
for swordfish.

In the bunkhouse in North Sydney
he shared a bottle of rum with a man
from Antigua. "The sea is like copper, oh yes,
and warm. The reef fish flicker yellow,
purple and green, coral feathers the tides."

Harvey's face white as the belly of a haddock.
His own too, likely. The many shades of black:
an oiled whetstone, the barrel
of a gun, the truth of his hammer in his hand.
Their house is in the middle of a field. The sheets
she brings in from the line spread
salt air and sunlight on the bed.

He builds woodsheds, houses, barns.

They eat the last of their bread and jerky,
blow on their fingers.
They've run out of easy things
to say, don't venture into other darknesses.

By dawn, he's drifting on a foreign sea. The trail
rises to meet him in a slow swell.
All the little cemeteries – the dead are adding up.
Did each one shovel and keep shovelling dirt
in the hope of clear water?

From the cape he sees the bay,
picks out a white dot, the house he built
in the middle of the field.

Two hours later he grunts goodbye to Harvey,
turns down his driveway, touches his wife and sons
as though he were a castaway.

Next day, on the staging
against a fish house,
he stands stolidly on the feet
that brought him back,
nails shingles to the wall.

# Mother-in-Law

The field heaves in slow swells, the house
as exposed as a Cape Islander: his idea to build

there. The floor's anchored by her oak table,
her squat refrigerator, the Enterprise stove

that burns birch he hauls from the back acres. She feeds
a circle of flame, with a singed newspaper rubs the stove,

its dark incandescence. As catalogue curtains hang limp
in the kitchen's tropical air, corned beef purls

through pools of fat; herring fillets jounce
in the cast-iron pan. Through the pantry window

she can hear the Rhode Island Reds by the barn,
their hubbubs of applause. Her motions clock-ruled

in a respectful universe, she gravitates around
mixing bowls, speckled navy roasters, the white hole

of the wringer washer. She clips sheets to a rope
line; over waves of hay, they luff and fill, crave

to be sewn to masts. When I tell her I have left
my husband, her eldest son, she asks no questions.

"Come home anytime, dear," she says. "You'll always
be welcome, you know that." I hadn't known. Years

of low, unadorned church hadn't prepared me
for grace. Summer after summer the borders

of the vegetable garden grow smaller. He drives her
to the wharf to watch the boats come in, to the dump

to watch for bears; she can't quite take for granted
store-bought jam, cabbages in May. Just once,

for his angina, she has to stay in the city. Exiled,
she looks like an X-ray of her own bones; or

like an animal who didn't make it on the Ark.
Of course there are potatoes with black rot

stored in her root cellar. I ask no questions.
Uncovetous of each other's lives, across

a most enlivening ignorance, we smile, she
punches down the sinewed dough, I elope to the beach.

In the dug well near the house, two brook trout swim
in circles, keeping the water clear, keeping it pure.

# Five Variations on an Enigma

## Many Years after Your Death

*for Ann, my sister,*
*whose name means grace*

Don't the scars on our bodies
matter? Between the lines in my palm

a punctuation mark neither turquoise
nor mauve, too blurred to end a sentence:

when I am five and you eleven, you stab me
with a pencil, consider me a worthy

enemy. Later, you wrestle with no one
but yourself, conceal your dislocations,

fold your voluptuous
feathers. Your shoulder blades,

at the last, are sharp as harrows
in thin, yellow soil: you grow

in your own way toward
your name, attentive to the blue

trumpets of morning glories,
honeysuckle's pale trombones.

You were my vanguard and my elder,
whole chapters of my story vanished with you.

Among the blemished leaves,
fragrance of pears, soft bedlam of the doves.

# In Dreams, I'm Always Searching for the Gate

The carpentry of sisterhood
a softwood fence; on your side,
untethered movements in the grass,

horses to gallop you into dangers
incompatible with those in houses, where
intimacy takes the bit between its teeth.

You hazard hoof-skid by a swollen
river; your horses amble you into joys
with the soil still on them:

a doe browsing
new leaves, each cluster
a green lily. You fall

ill in the season of distinctive
warblers and wet cedar. As the gate
swings open, you're running

your words together, revelations
spill from you. In the hospital,
you order my lover to take care of me.

At home, curbed, you watch
your favourite mare through
the window, her coat coiled smoke

like that of the stallion who rears
*Santiago El Grande,* a naked saint,
toward a flock of faded angels.

## Counterpoint

During the war, we stole cheese rinds
    from the larder's stone shelves;
the wooden spoon our mother used for spanking

mixed starch in a big china bowl. Her Edwardian
    pearls. After her last stroke, only her eyes
moved. Your daughter's born, umbilical cord

around her throat. You feed her at your breast, pat her
    when she cries. You dust the dark oak chairs, you know
every room intimately. The *gronk* of ring-necked pheasants

stealing seedlings from your garden. Where
    would you contradict me? It pleased you, you say,
to polish the piano, scent of lemons

and a jade-green bowl – your fingernail making
    the glass sing. You grow sweet peas, their fragrant
paintbox colours, and pansies with sober

two-dimensional faces. Often you wear dark glasses
    indoors, like the blackout curtains that concealed us
from attack (cancer cells thrive on division,

don't understand they need a living body).
    Escaping to the stables, you curry your horses;
dust twirls in the air, partnered with light.

I'm reading a Russian poet who says
    better to leave life without clinging to even
a shadow on the wall – your back bent, the horse's

ponderous curves. The poet hanged herself
    the year I was born: we're such amateurs
with our pretty calendars on our walls. Now, when I pass

your house, the pines you planted hide the steps
    where you were carried to the ambulance
that morning, the arches of your feet like abalone.

Our mother's eyes were caged
    blue foxes. Your family was asleep
when you sat up in bed, swallowed pills one

by one, lay down again. You'd handwritten
    your instructions: body to science,
no funeral, cremation and a common grave –

you shall have knives and fire and no singing.
    The Russian poet says that to conquer time,
we must pass without a trace. I praise cotyledons

and tendrils, the great bowls of your horses' hips;
    and when I meet you, or you, on the street,
I raise dark glasses so you can see my eyes.

## In the Kitchen

Late in the year I move
a long way from home, from
the often unvisited

headstones of my family. I take out
your recipe for citrus mousse
handwritten in a letter...see you

on the sixteenth. Do we reach
with the same gesture
for the orange juice?

Clotted heap of whipped cream,
sleek egg white, every colour but blue
beaten from it. And I,

domesticated, incorporate
this air. Write to me, you say.
Write to me.

## Coda

Years after my sister's death, her daughter
and I travel to a funeral. We're wearing black,
my jacket fuchsia, hers burnt
orange. Afterward, we drive north

to the beach. It's a day for children:
blue sky, green fields, flocks of
dandelions. Great blue herons
in a cove, their antiquated

patience, the throat of one tumoured
with a living fish. It's a day for the dying.
Grey wings scattering light's
silver scales. Winter rye in rows

of undotted *i's*. The black paws
of a red fox. She asks about her mother's
illness. I tell her what I remember. Then
I tell her about the portrait I saw years ago

at my uncle's house in Surrey: head
of a Japanese man surrounded by red and purple
anemones. And how, recently, I saw the painting
again. Around the man's head are seedpods

of lotus, sienna and mud-brown,
oriental characters elusive as salamanders:
it's a day for memory, for chameleon
and shaman. We take off our shoes,

shed our jackets, spread our arms
like the wings of cormorants. It's a day
for my niece and me. Orange and pink
banners. The white breakage of ocean.

haiku for a dreaming dog

first time at the beach —
rushing toward each other
  dog and wave

# Tooth of the Lion

I walk through the orchard with my grandson; he wades
waist-deep in dandelions; picks them and always

there are more; sits on them, watches as the unbroken
lever themselves upright; tosses them, comets through blue space

he unseats the bees
I braid him a crown
our fingertips
drenched with gold

later, the grass littered with grey windfalls, he holds
a stem like a wand and blows, laughing

as seeds tear free; they wander
liminal, like pilgrims

# Gift of a Day

*It was passed from one bird to another,*
*the whole gift of a day.*
*The day went from flute to flute,*
*went dressed in vegetation…*

"Bird"

Pablo Neruda

When do they touch?
Wild geese forming V's
are saviours of distance.
Flights of swallows
collared against encounter;
one tern's imperious hover.
Pointillism of wind: those
flocked starlings. And yet –
though this is how they manoeuvre –
*it was passed from one bird to another*

by sleight of wing, was never
dropped: the plumule
of desire. When swallows immigrate
too soon, they're driven low
to ricochet off rivers.
Don't think this is display.
Desire – expecting from the stars –
bolts desperation whole,
cannot treat as cliché
*the whole gift of a day.*

The gift was holy, the day
a stopover between migrations
(flying from the north, black-
bellied plovers scatter
the feathers of their name).
The magnitude of the assault!
Nestlings night-stunned under down,
dialects of sparrows in dispute.
In hollowed bones the song was sought.
*The day went from flute to flute,*

went for its sky-tumbled, leaf-
braked ride: the tunnels through
the branches caving in with green.
Barn swallows are laughter
on the wing, cinnamon
and the tranced air's reunion
wrapping the blue-green shoulders
of the world. The day, all day,
in sweetness breathed out oxygen,
*went dressed in vegetation.*

I want to read this to you

Is the language of happiness
agile, or does it curl up
on warm sand, listening
to a wave collapse?
                    The dip
above your collarbone
a tidal pool: my separate life
disappears, reappears. Wet
fingers, your breastbone's
sheen of flesh: *essential*
contains *to be* in all its tenses
of possibility and loss.

# From the telephone by the lake

I get sound waves,
inflections, your rare
laughter, my fingers curl
around plastic anchored
to the staff house wall
where a bulb burns day
and night, where moths cling dazed
or spellbound, cream wings lapped
in dusky rose, bodies furred pale
as pollen. A June bug ricochets,
lacquered, cracked open.
The metal hammock
bent against the rail, did it ever
sway to a south wind? I walk back
to my cabin through the wavering circles
of my flashlight, through
witherod and wild columbine, flickering
bats. Somewhere I read
that for an ancient Greek to be called
stoic he must in silence
clasp a live fox
to his belly. I hold to my face
the shirt I took warm from your body
the morning I left.

I'll tell you a story...

You stumble from your winter den. Blinking,
stunned by light. And hungry. Hungry.

The lath-boned dogs of Trinidad,
where you were born. You ran with them

for years, forgot your cousin Halcyon:
named for a kingfisher that nests at

winter solstice, calms with its mythic wings
the darkened seas. I lift a moonshell

to my ear, it whispers *holdfast,*
*fulmar.* My body's gone

that once was curled to fit
its safety. How do we map

the contour lines of trust: dead-leaf rustle,
trestle over whitewater? *Ceryle alcyon*

dives for minnows, dives to escape
the peregrine. I swim through

the currents in your voice, through tender
reeds. Are you a river or a lake?

# Estuary

They've been waiting some time, although neither
would have used the word *waiting*.

The river slides through sand; the ocean drawn
shallow, its ambivalence, monotonous obsequies.

*Estuary* a word left by the tide. He considers
the mingling of waters (the sea turns toward

darkness, the river pulled with it). She thinks, frith
of dilution. How long since she'd so much to lose?

They're held by the gaunt sphere of reflection,
of menses and tides (the mutable shapeliness,

warm waters of flesh). Slow wakening to morning,
luna moths clinging to the knives of the willows.

Staring into the light, from their sundial of footprints,
fingernails torn from rebraiding old cords,

she thinks, *brine* means *to burn;* he thinks,
crèche of the eiders. Under filleted clouds, they assay

the word *love;* they're acquainted with turbulence,
with delicate exchanges of water and salt.

If time is the river? If desire is the ocean? They fear
the reverse, for neither is young. They watch ospreys,

bone-breakers, climb the arduous cliffs of the air.
They watch terns link antipodal light.

# The Coldest December in Years

I'm living with you now, far
from home, neither of us quite prepared
to trust this fourth, this seventh
chance. The wind's snagged
in the crystalled dogwood, astonished
by the possibilities
of stillness; and owls
have lost all warm-blooded
memory of how to hunt, are clipped
invisibly to the high branches of
cottonwoods, the blackened
amputations of bur
oaks. Should I walk the fields
as far as that farm
enclosed in fir and willow?
There's all the room in the world here
for emptiness. The low sun melts
nothing.
       I'm told
the river froze high, then
subsided. Devotion, ankled
in soft feathers, impels me
to tramp this thieving
brilliant cold,
         as trapped air
echoes water forging north.
You have allowed me to enter
the auricles of your solitude.

# When It Alteration Finds

Heated words, the pale fleece
of my breathing. I leave the car, cross

the ditch. I'm surrounded by prairie,
by snow without shadow (at night

a few lights scattered like a fleet of trawlers).
A grove of trees is called a bluff, reed grass

Christ's teeth, each blade marred
as though incisors had clamped on a cry.

I'm more attuned to the polyphony
of coves, a limpid turquoise buoyancy

and the nag of foam (July's canola brazen
as a gong, fields of flax not quite committed

to blue, cool enough to swim in; a sky
full of misguided action: winter domain

of the rough-legged hawk, marked at each wrist
like a manacle). No, to the four directions, to four

of the five senses: landscape for the colour-blind,
who invent eleven words for grey. How long

must I stand here before I smell voles
in their crooked tunnels, taste the wing-

scrape of a snowy owl, feel
the small punches of your pulse?

Landscape of introversion, the singular
necessary other. My boots breaking the crust,

I head out across the field, the horizon
a polished bone cleansed of the tongue's

approximations, of gestures like
grey's assumption of cirrus-white.

Landscape of black clay weighted
with floods and sunflowers – aren't

prepositions bees swarming the word *love?*
I turn around. You're standing by the car,

watching me. I step into the hollows
that I made, toe to heel and

heel to toe, and when I reach you,
we clasp each other's wrists

until our fingers warm;
then we drive on.

# Second Anniversary

The rooms I scrubbed and waxed
for our beginning
weave dust among grey hairs.
Spiders join us, and fruit flies

so light our wrists don't register
their landings. I kill
your jade plant by overwatering. You drop
my favourite mug, blue iris

severed from the stem. We fashion
brief tranquilities,
and recollect. How the foghorn
saturates the mist! We're wading

tall grass prairie, where inklings
are hidden like
gentians. We are not in the fear
of God. My arms overflowing

with purple lilac, their wandering plumes
of scent, is this
what frightens you? There's no insurance
in this city against flood; if you ask,

they laugh at you. Aren't we offering
each other
our small perimeters − *listen,*
*like a robin, to what moves*

*below the grass.* We want to be
open windows,
through which heat can enter and
the kind of rain that makes leaves

flinch. I slice open nectarines,
their skin
flushed, flesh softening. With a dull
blade, you scrape scales from a wild

salmon. On the shelves,
our books gradually mingle.

# Sable Island

*44°N 60°W*

the island bends
to current, wind and wave,
                                 marram grass
netting the dunes, which bury and disinter
seal rib, sparrow rib, rib of a feral horse
        arc of a dolphin's spine, sand
where the heart was

at dusk, a yearling's carcass
            taints the air,
the mare's first foal shivers in the wind,
its legs buckling, while

                       grey seals
enter the ocean single-minded as sperm,
            in water their bodies flow
like water, and from the waves they watch you
tread unstable sand
in which garnets are ground small

at dawn, the mare lowers her head to her dead foal,
kicks at the stallion who's nudging her along

later she wanders off to graze, wades
the western ponds

        the foal moors a small dune

curve to your own mortality, see how
grasses grow through an empty hoof
           and watch the migrant finch, its feathers
           the blue of ocean, intensified
as a lens bends
sunlight to burning

# After getting the test results

he's walking home. Along the shore,
herring gulls circle refuse; they're immaculate,

as if they soared the Labrador Current.
A moth steers a feckless course between

raindrops. As for that pigeon he just startled,
its jadeite throat's a game for three players: white light,

barbed feathers and his eye: the possibilities
inside every plain statement. Crows mob him;

he sees a fledgling on the grass, its spasmodic
heaves for air, and tries to walk past

that moment when *arbitrary* quits the vein,
enters the heart. Why bother finding a puddle

that says *this is how you look*. He's more
than his body, which now has him pitilessly

in its sights. He slows down. His street. This
is his house. He has to go inside; they're waiting.

In his garden, a bumblebee staggers
through canyons of gold crocuses.

## From a Window

On the corner
a woman in a gold jacket. I glance
down at the page,
look up, she's gone.
The density peculiar to each of us.
Where her gold jacket blocked
the view, far down the street
forsythia in bloom. Daily
we walk on concrete, the city
a headstone without
inscription. Yellow petals
can hold only so much rain.

# Under Glass in the Winnipeg Art Gallery

*Douwan, widow of a prince, daughter-*
*and sister-in-law of emperors*

        A jade plug
for each orifice, a jade
cicada upon your tongue, your body
wrapped in silk, dressed
in a suit of jade. Two thousand tiles
knotted with gold, a hole
at the crown for your soul
to slip through.
           Encased in 100,000 days
of backaches, you were entombed
in a bald mountain. Could the carvers
with their treadles and quartz sand
grind their way into Heaven?
Did just one widow risk
the hide whips to place a cicada
on her husband's tongue?

After your husband died, you threw
his eighteen-sided dice
down the privy; dreamed of drowning
his concubines in molten iron. The evening
you were measured for your suit, you drank
soup made from the nests of birds. When
the carvers were finished, you skirted
lanterns and watchmen, clambered up on the bench,
slid your legs into the trousers. Small rectangles
imprinted on the backs of your thighs.

Did you ever notice how carp
polish the water of a pool? How
the white petals of peonies lean
backward, like a face laid open to grief?

*two thousand years later, an iron door*
*breached*
        *two thousand tiles stained*
*with the Princess Douwan*

If you could do it again, would you go
to old Chen, pay him to coax
your likeness from a lump
of green stone? Your head tilted
as the emperor reads
one of his poems, your long sleeves
quiet as a river.

# On the Plains of the Indus

*[2143 BCE]*

I climb mud steps
to the ramparts. Mohenjo-daro,
city of brick. Five years
I worked the kilns, where any memory
of water was driven from clay.

I tilt my head back. Black flood plain, a fever
of stars: leaping tiger, coiled snake, elephant in *musth*
who breaks the laws of his own herd. My prayer
dies on my tongue.
Moon Woman watches me, her sadness
increasing. Three nights she must lie
in River's bed, held down
by Crocodile.
          Her shadows sharp
in the high-walled lanes, on the square houses.
Odour creeps through the drains.
Granary and citadel, the great bath, jungle
falling back to feed the fires.

The main streets offer North Wind
no hindrance. Skulls in their boxes
of scented rosewood point north, souls
blown south to the sea: which I picture
as a great flood that never loosens its hold.

What does the river know that I have missed?

I've lived nineteen monsoons, she
fifteen. Our child kicks
hard in her belly's half-moon. I smell
her fear.
In the evenings I bring clay home, shape
a toy bullock-cart, two dancing
boars. They make her laugh.
Her bracelets jingle.

Today the oldest man in Mohenjo-daro
died. Thirty-four times
he'd circled the seasons. The ribs of the unborn
curve to a narrow valley of bone.

The overseer found my sketch
of the madman
pissing in a turban; looked
thoughtful, went away. Now
I'm apprenticed, engraving
soapstone seals
that fit the palm of the hand,
make impressions in clay.

I practice. Inscriptions first: *water-holder;*
*the singer's mark; belonging to Munala, mistress*
*of one hundred ploughed fields.*

Then gazelles, peacocks, goats,
the zebu bull. My chisels and drills
soon blunted, my discards
marking bales, claiming goods, naming
families. Her time
closer. Moon Woman dissolves in the sky.

My seals grow smaller, could be cupped by a child.

I carve a figure with three
faces. His horns
and horned erection hold at bay
the tiger's claws.

I carve a woman, her thighs parted.
From her womb grows a pipal tree,
sacred fig that links
River's gift of earth with the white crane's flight.

I disobey decree, take these seals home
in the cotton folds of my turban, give them to her
just before sundown.
                    She falls asleep
holding them.

Grief, from the Latin, *gravis*;
chrysalis, from the Greek for gold

Mourning: a chrysalis? A question you can ask
only when you have dissolved
into the answer. Why wouldn't we be unwilling

pupils of grief: raw stone of the *cordillera*,
its desperate inversions. Inconceivable
that butterflies emerge like princes

of orange, caparisoned. Watch them tumble
the slopes, fall mile upon mile to
the *oyamel* pines of Angangueo. Lighting

in their thousands, they bend
branches. Do they forget rain's terrible
glue, mice that scissor the wings

from the body? Step closer, warm them
with your breath. They will rise
into the air like soft applause.

## Under a Trembling Aspen

It's November. I'm walking
east on Churchill Drive toward a car
parked under a tree. In the passenger seat,
wearing his seat belt, a plaid rug
over his knees,
is
a life-size statue of the Buddha.
His topknot's
like a cluster of Concord grapes.
I smile at the Buddha.
The Buddha smiles back. Or is he smiling
at the St. Vital Bridge? The whole
western sky?

The car's in front of a stucco
bungalow. The Dhammapada
says you split ridgepoles
and rafters, I tell him,
no wonder
you've been left
outside. But if
you're here
to stay, someone
should buy you a saffron
parka. As for the Schubert
chokecherry, the green
ash, the brown waters
of the river, they're all
one to you: the delta,
the lake, the bay's belugas
with their enigmatic
smiles. Could moments
of compassion in
the city of
Winnipeg add up to
one bodhisattva?
                    Today
you're driven
on the four wheels
of appetite. Will you
panhandle

And years ago
I brought in frozen
T-shirts and pyjamas
from the clothesline,
hung them
on a rack
in the kitchen of the old
farmhouse in Horton's
Landing. I'm alone
in the house. I
go upstairs, come
back down, the rack
is rocking back
and forth and I'm grinning
widely — *so poltergeists
are real* — when from behind
my son's blue
jeans a barn
cat leaps to the floor
streaks for the back
porch,
            and I'm walking
the dunes of
Lake Winnipeg in
October when I see
how the wind and three
long,

in Osborne Village,
be borne aloft
from a three-car garage
in Tuxedo?
I've always
admired the way
you died, lying
down without fuss
among the sal trees.
Yesterday I copied
a phrase from *Prairie
Fire:* "this high teaching
of daily decency." Please
would you raise
one crudely molded
hand
     in blessing?

recumbent,
dried-up
blades of grass
have incised in the sand
perfect concentric circles,
a mandala,
       and when I give
birth, fulfillment
harpstrings
my soles
to my crown,
and
    right now
over my head
the Leonid shower
is happening
      at noon.

# Notes

"Latticework"
The remark about images, as told to Tu Fu, is found in *Twentieth Century Pleasures,* by Robert Hass (The Ecco Press).

"In Alabaster for the Palace of the King of Assyria"
The sculptures of the lion hunts of Ashurbanipal, for his palace built in Nineveh about 645 BCE, are located in the British Museum.

"A Few Days after the Whirlwind"
I am indebted to Stephen Mitchell's translation, *The Book of JOB* (North Point Press), for the names of Job's daughters. As Ilana Pardes points out in *Countertraditions in the Bible* (Harvard University Press), this is the sole biblical record of a father actually naming his daughters.

"Ear to the Ground"
The quotation in section 1 is from *Requiem 1935-1940,* by Anna Akhmatova (Selected Poems, Harvill).

"Composed in Exile"
Giya Kancheli was born in Georgia in 1935; since 1992 he has spent most of his time in Berlin.
*Domine, exaudi vocem meam...* Lord, hear my voice.
*Abii me videram...* I turned away so as not to see.

"Locked-In Syndrome"
In 1995 Jean-Dominique Bauby suffered a massive stroke that left him paralysed, able to move only his left eyelid. In July and August of 1996, he wrote *The Diving-Bell and the Butterfly* (Fourth Estate); and in the same year set up ALIS (Association du Locked-In Syndrome). He died in 1997.

"In Dreams, I'm Always Searching for the Gate"
The painting *Santiago El Grande,* by Salvador Dali, is found in the Beaverbrook Art Gallery, Fredericton, NB.

"Counterpoint"
The Russian poet is Marina Tsvetayeva, 1892-1941. The particular poem is quoted in Paul Auster's *Invention of Solitude* (Penguin Books).
The ashes of those who donate their bodies to Dalhousie University are interred in a common grave.

"Gift of a Day"
The four lines by Neruda are from *Fully Empowered* (New Directions Books), and were translated by Alastair Reid.

"Under Glass in the Winnipeg Art Gallery"
The use of jade burial suits for members of the imperial court characterized the Han dynasty (206 BCE to 220 CE).

"On the Plains of the Indus"
     The Indus Valley civilization extended from about 2500 BCE to 1700 BCE.
     I am indebted to the article by Walter A. Fairservis, Jr., in *Scientific American*,
     March 1983, Volume 248, Number 3, "The Script of the Indus Valley
     Civilization," for the inscriptions. The two seals I have described are among
     the best-known artefacts of this civilization.

"Under a Trembling Aspen"
     The quotation is from *Prairie Fire: Vol. 21 No. 1.*

"Sable Island" is for Zoe Lucas.

"After getting the test results" is in memory of Jimmie MacLean, 1942-1999.



## Acknowledgements

A number of these poems have appeared, some in earlier versions, in *The
Fiddlehead, TickleAce, Pottersfield Portfolio, The Malahat Review, Grain, The Antigonish
Review, PRISM International, Event, Prairie Fire* and *CV2*. I am grateful to the
editors.

At the Atlantic School of Theology, the Reverend Dr. Shelley Davis Finson and
Dr. Susan Slater guided me with humour and insight into feminist theology and
the Hebrew Scriptures.

My thanks to the poetry group in Halifax for thoughtful criticism that combined
honesty with care. Special thanks to Sue MacLeod and Margo Wheaton for reading
the manuscript; to Brian Bartlett, a generous teacher of poetry-writing at St.
Mary's University; and to Sandra Barry, for steadfast encouragement.

During the past two years, George Amabile has become poetry mentor, editor and
friend; in many ways, this book owes its existence to him.

Without Barbara Markovits, Mary Jo Anderson, Anne Hicks and Michael
Hundiak, I might not have had faith in those first, long-ago poems, let alone in a
book. My particular thanks to Mary Jo for her thoughts on the final section.

Lastly, I am grateful to Dr. Gavin Hanke of The Manitoba Museum for his kindness
in lending the nest and egg that were photographed for the cover.